GW00383370

To

_____

From

_____

Date

_____

My Little Book on God

© 2005 Christian Art Gifts, RSA
           Christian Art Gifts Inc., IL, USA

Compiled by Lynette Douglas
Designed by Christian Art Gifts

Printed in China

ISBN 1-86920-540-5

05   06   07   08   09   10   11   12   13   14   –   10 9 8 7 6 5 4 3

My
LITTLE
BOOK on
GOD

christian
art gifts

CONTENTS

GOD

God (gɒd) *n* 1 The sole Supreme Being, eternal, spiritual, and transcendent. He is the Creator and ruler of all and is infinite in all attributes; the object of worship in monotheistic religions.

Collins Dictionary

Then the LORD came down in the cloud
and stood there with him
and proclaimed his name, the LORD.
And he passed in front of Moses,
proclaiming, "The LORD, the LORD,
the compassionate and gracious God,
slow to anger, abounding in love
and faithfulness, maintaining love
to thousands, and forgiving wickedness,
rebellion and sin."

~ Exodus 34:5-7 ~

INTRODUCTION

We worship and serve the almighty God, the One who revealed Himself to Moses as I AM WHO I AM. He is the only true God, the Lord of Hosts.

Each time He interacted in a new way with one of His servants, He gave us a glimpse of a new facet of His glory and majesty, a new insight into the magnificence of His character. That is why the Bible gives so many titles for God.

This little book takes some of the many names of God and ponders on them. Scripture verses then draw our focus more fully to the splendor of our God, and a quote inspires us to worship our awesome God.

GOD IS CREATOR

Elohim

In the beginning
God created the heavens
and the earth.
~ Genesis 1:1 ~

Creator

God created a beautiful world – and God saw that it was good. He was pleased with what He had made – and then He gave us the world and all its beauty to enjoy. Each day we can find pleasure in His creativity and enjoy His glorious splendor.

Wherever we look there is evidence of the greatness of God. His creativity is endless: each sunset has its own delightful radiance, each flower its distinctive loveliness.

God has created such variety and splendor to remind us of His infinite glory.

From His Word

The heavens declare the glory of God; the skies proclaim the work of his hands.

Psalm 19:1

You alone are the LORD. You made the heavens, even the highest heavens, and all their starry host, the earth and all that is on it, the seas and all that is in them. You give life to everything, and the multitudes of heaven worship you.

Nehemiah 9:6

Blessed is he whose help is the God of Jacob, whose hope is in the LORD his God, the Maker of heaven and earth, the sea, and everything in them – the LORD, who remains faithful forever.

Psalm 146:5-6

The earth is the LORD's, and everything in it, the world, and all who live in it; for he founded it upon the seas and established it upon the waters.

Psalm 24:1-2

Creator

"You are worthy, our Lord and God, to receive glory and honor and power, for you created all things, and by your will they were created and have their being."

Revelation 4:11

Ah, Sovereign LORD, you have made the heavens and the earth by your great power and outstretched arm. Nothing is too hard for you.

Jeremiah 32:17

All things bright and beautiful,
All creatures great and small,
All things wise and wonderful,
The Lord God made them all.

Cecil Frances Alexander

GOD IS ALMIGHTY

El Shaddai

Jesus looked at them and said,
"With man this is impossible,
but with God all things are possible."

~ Matthew 19:26 ~

Almighty

God is able to handle any situation, because He is almighty and all-sufficient.

Nobody is stronger than God.

Nobody is more powerful. He can do anything and everything necessary to look after you.

Nothing is impossible for God.

El Shaddai is able to meet all your needs and He will fulfill His promises to you in His perfect time and way. What seems impossible to you is more than possible to Him.

From His Word

After this I heard what sounded like the roar of a great multitude in heaven shouting: "Hallelujah! Salvation and glory and power belong to our God."

Revelation 19:1

Finally, be strong in the Lord and in his mighty power. Put on the full armor of God so that you can take your stand against the devil's schemes.

Ephesians 6:10-11

You, dear children, are from God and have overcome them, because the one who is in you is greater than the one who is in the world.

1 John 4:4

O LORD God Almighty, who is like you? You are mighty, O Lord, and your faithfulness surrounds you.

Psalm 89:8

Almighty

I know that you can do all things; no plan of yours can be thwarted.

Job 42:2

Ah, Sovereign LORD, you have made the heavens and the earth by your great power and outstretched arm. Nothing is too hard for you.

Jeremiah 32:17

The God of the Bible is the God who reveals Himself in all the glory and the wonder of His miraculous eternal power.

Martyn Lloyd-Jones

GOD IS HOLY

Who will not fear you, O Lord,
and bring glory to your name?
For you alone are holy.
All nations will come and worship
before you, for your righteous
acts have been revealed.

~ Revelation 15:4 ~

Holy

God is absolutely pure and perfect. There is nothing in Him that is in any way deceitful or even hints of evil or wrongdoing. Everything He does is done in righteousness. He is the Holy One; morally perfect and fully virtuous, honorable and upright.

Everything God does is faultless and just. His holiness defines His divinity and we can confidently trust that He will always do what is right and good.

From His Word

And they were calling to one another: "Holy, holy, holy is the LORD Almighty; the whole earth is full of his glory."

Isaiah 6:3

This is the message we have heard from him and declare to you: God is light; in him there is no darkness at all.

1 John 1:5

Since we have these promises, dear friends, let us purify ourselves from everything that contaminates body and spirit, perfecting holiness out of reverence for God.

2 Corinthians 7:1

Such a high priest meets our need – one who is holy, blameless, pure, set apart from sinners, exalted above the heavens.

Hebrews 7:26

Holy

I am the LORD your God; consecrate yourselves
and be holy, because I am holy.

Leviticus 11:44

Your eyes are too pure to look on evil; you cannot
tolerate wrong.

Habakkuk 1:13

Every good and perfect gift is from above, coming
down from the Father of the heavenly lights, who
does not change like shifting shadows.

James 1:17

Real holiness has love for its essence, humility
for its clothing, the good of others as its em-
ployment, and the honor of God as its end.

Nathanael Emmons

OUR PROVIDER

Jehovah Jireh

So Abraham called that place
The LORD Will Provide.
And to this day it is said,
"On the mountain of the LORD
it will be provided."

~ Genesis 22:14 ~

Provider

God knows what His children need and promises to provide everything that is necessary for us to live a godly life.

He is deeply compassionate and extravagantly generous. He has more than enough for all our needs, and we can always trust Him to do what is best for us.

Do you need comfort? God is the Comforter. Do you need guidance? He sends His Holy Spirit to show us the way.

Do you need righteousness? He provided it through the blood of Jesus Christ.

Do you need wisdom? He is our wisdom. Trust Him. He will give you what you need. Always.

From His Word

He who did not spare his own Son, but gave him up for us all – how will he not also, along with him, graciously give us all things?

Romans 8:32

"For the pagans run after all these things, and your heavenly Father knows that you need them. But seek first his kingdom and his righteousness, and all these things will be given to you as well."

Matthew 6:32-33

And my God will meet all your needs according to his glorious riches in Christ Jesus.

Philippians 4:19

May God give you of heaven's dew and of earth's richness an abundance of grain and new wine.

Genesis 27:28

Delight yourself in the LORD and he will give you the desires of your heart.

Psalm 37:4

Provider

Taste and see that the LORD is good; blessed is the man who takes refuge in him. Fear the LORD, you his saints, for those who fear him lack nothing. The lions may grow weak and hungry, but those who seek the LORD lack no good thing.

Psalm 34:8-10

Command those who are rich in this present world not to be arrogant nor to put their hope in wealth, which is so uncertain, but to put their hope in God, who richly provides us with everything for our enjoyment.

1 Timothy 6:17

How blessed and wonderful, beloved, are the gifts of God. Life in immortality, splendor in righteousness, truth in perfect confidence, faith in assurance, self-control in holiness!

Clement

OUR RIGHTEOUSNESS

Jehovah Tsidkenu

This is the name
by which he will be called:
The LORD Our Righteousness.
~ Jeremiah 23:6 ~

Righteousness

God is upright, just and holy. But the greatest wonder of all is that He has made it possible for us to be holy, too.

No matter how hard we try we will always fall short of the perfection of God, but He loves us so much that He didn't want to live without us.

That is why He sent Christ to make a way for us to become righteous. Because we are now righteous through His blood, we can live forever in His presence.

As we confess our sins, God blots them out, and removes the stain of sin in our lives. In Him, we too can be holy and righteous.

From His Word

"Holy, holy, holy is the LORD Almighty; the whole earth is full of his glory."

Isaiah 6:3

Who will not fear you, O Lord, and bring glory to your name? For you alone are holy. All nations will come and worship before you, for your righteous acts have been revealed.

Revelation 15:4

God made him who had no sin to be sin for us, so that in him we might become the righteousness of God.

2 Corinthians 5:21

He is the Rock, his works are perfect, and all his ways are just. A faithful God who does no wrong, upright and just is he.

Deuteronomy 32:4

Righteousness

"Who among the gods is like you, O Lord? Who is like you – majestic in holiness, awesome in glory, working wonders?"

Exodus 15:11

I am the Lord your God; consecrate yourselves and be holy, because I am holy.

Leviticus 11:44

Your eyes are too pure to look on evil; you cannot tolerate wrong.

Habakkuk 1:13

My hope is built on nothing less
than Jesus' blood and righteousness.

Edward Mote

GOD IS MY BANNER

Jehovah Nissi

Moses built an altar
and called it
"The LORD is my Banner."
~ Exodus 17:15 ~

Banner

The Bible tells us that God is the commanding officer of the hosts of heaven, the leader of the army of the Almighty.

God is always victorious, always triumphant, and always the winner! We are on the winning side, even when it feels as if we are losing every battle.

As you read the Bible you will see that God overcomes evil. His truth and goodness will prevail. And we will live as more than conquerors because of what He has done for us.

From His Word

For the LORD your God is the one who goes with you to fight for you against your enemies to give you victory.

Deuteronomy 20:4

You give me your shield of victory, and your right hand sustains me; you stoop down to make me great.

Psalm 18:35

We will shout for joy when you are victorious and will lift up our banners in the name of our God. May the LORD grant all your requests.

Psalm 20:5

In your majesty ride forth victoriously in behalf of truth, humility and righteousness; let your right hand display awesome deeds.

Psalm 45:4

Banner

With God we will gain the victory, and he will trample down our enemies.

Psalm 60:12

The LORD will march out like a mighty man, like a warrior he will stir up his zeal; with a shout he will raise the battle cry and will triumph over his enemies.

Isaiah 42:13

And having disarmed the powers and authorities, he made a public spectacle of them, triumphing over them by the cross.

Colossians 2:15

> The most important of life's battles is the one we fight daily in the silent chambers of the soul.
>
> David O. McKay

GOD IS OUR HEALER

Jehovah Rapha

"I am the LORD, who heals you."
~ Exodus 15:26 ~

Healer

God cares about our physical condition, just as He cares about our spiritual condition. The Bible is filled with stories of God's healing touch in the lives of sick people.

Therefore, we can and should pray, asking God to touch us in our illnesses. However, we should understand that healing does not always occur in dramatic ways.

Sometimes it is a slow process of recovery that allows time to pray and focus on spiritual well-being.

Sometimes there is even death, but then we must remember that death is simply a doorway to eternal health and wholeness!

From His Word

Praise the LORD, O my soul, and forget not all his benefits – who forgives all your sins and heals all your diseases.

Psalm 103:2-3

He sent forth his word and healed them; he rescued them from the grave.

Psalm 107:20

Jesus went throughout Galilee, teaching in their synagogues, preaching the good news of the kingdom, and healing every disease and sickness among the people.

Matthew 4:23

Heal me, O LORD, and I will be healed; save me and I will be saved, for you are the one I praise.

Jeremiah 17:14

He heals the brokenhearted and binds up their wounds.

Psalm 147:3

Healer

Remember your word to your servant, for you have given me hope. My comfort in my suffering is this: Your promise preserves my life.

Psalm 119:49-50

O LORD my God, I called to you for help and you healed me.

Psalm 30:2

He himself bore our sins in his body on the tree, so that we might die to sins and live for righteousness; by his wounds you have been healed.

1 Peter 2:24

In tribulation, immediately draw near to God with trust, and you will receive strength, enlightenment and instruction.

John of the Cross

GOD IS PEACE

Jehovah Shalom

So Gideon built an altar
to the LORD there and called it
"The LORD is Peace."
~ Judges 6:24 ~

Peace

Peace is not an external absence of conflict but an inner sense of assurance that all will be well because your heavenly Father cares for you.

The God of peace is in control of the world and when we submit to Him and live as He calls us to, we will experience peace even when everything around us is in chaos.

Too often we worry because we haven't yet learned to trust God in all things and so we deprive ourselves of peace.

Lay all your worries and concerns at His feet today, and you will experience His peace that passes all understanding.

From His Word

You will keep in perfect peace him whose mind is steadfast, because he trusts in you.

Isaiah 26:3

Therefore, since we have been justified through faith, we have peace with God through our Lord Jesus Christ.

Romans 5:1

May the God of hope fill you with all joy and peace as you trust in him, so that you may overflow with hope by the power of the Holy Spirit.

Romans 15:13

Let the peace of Christ rule in your hearts, since as members of one body you were called to peace.

Colossians 3:15

The LORD gives strength to his people; the LORD blesses his people with peace.

Psalm 29:11

Peace

Now may the Lord of peace himself give you peace at all times and in every way. The Lord be with all of you.

2 Thessalonians 3:16

For he himself is our peace, who has made the two one and has destroyed the barrier, the dividing wall of hostility, by abolishing in his flesh the law with its commandments and regulations.

Ephesians 2:14-15

If God be our God He will give us peace in trouble. When there is a storm without, He will make peace within. The world can create trouble in peace, but God can create peace in trouble.

Thomas Watson

GOD IS MY SHEPHERD

Jehovah Rohi

The LORD is my shepherd,
I shall not be in want.
~ Psalm 23:1 ~

Shepherd

God is a God of grace and compassion. He is always dependable, always faithful, always constant.

We can count on Him always to come through for us, always protect us, always guide us and always lead us to safety.

With His rod He fights off our enemy and with His staff He gently leads us along the paths of righteousness.

What joy it is to know that He nurtures us, loves us and provides for us always.

From His Word

Hear us, O Shepherd of Israel, you who lead Joseph like a flock; you who sit enthroned between the cherubim, shine forth.

Psalm 80:1

He will stand and shepherd his flock in the strength of the LORD, in the majesty of the name of the LORD his God. And they will live securely, for then his greatness will reach to the ends of the earth.

Micah 5:4

He tends his flock like a shepherd: He gathers the lambs in his arms and carries them close to his heart; he gently leads those that have young.

Isaiah 40:11

Then I will give you shepherds after my own heart, who will lead you with knowledge and understanding.

Jeremiah 3:15

Shepherd

"Hear the word of the LORD, O nations; proclaim it in distant coastlands: 'He who scattered Israel will gather them and will watch over his flock like a shepherd.'"

Jeremiah 31:10

May the God of peace, who through the blood of the eternal covenant brought back from the dead our Lord Jesus, that great Shepherd of the sheep.

Hebrews 13:20

The King of love my Shepherd is,
Whose goodness faileth never;
I nothing lack if I am His
And He is mine forever.

Henry Williams Baker

GOD IS ETERNAL

El Olam

Abraham planted a tamarisk tree
in Beersheba, and there
he called upon the name
of the LORD, the Eternal God.

~ Genesis 21:33 ~

Eternal

God is eternal and infinite. He has no beginning and no end. He has no limits and He does not change. He sees the end from the beginning and He will work all things out for our benefit and for His glory.

He is Lord forever – He has ruled from the beginning and will do so until the end of time and through all eternity.

We are bound by time, but God is not bound by anything. The things that concern us now, He sees from the perspective of eternity. And that is why we need never worry, but can trust Him always and in all things.

From His Word

Now to the King eternal, immortal, invisible, the only God, be honor and glory for ever and ever. Amen.

1 Timothy 1:17

God, the blessed and only Ruler, the King of kings and Lord of lords, who alone is immortal and who lives in unapproachable light, whom no one has seen or can see. To him be honor and might forever. Amen.

1 Timothy 6:15-16

Before the mountains were born or you brought forth the earth and the world, from everlasting to everlasting you are God.

Psalm 90:2

But from everlasting to everlasting the LORD's love is with those who fear him, and his righteousness with their children's children.

Psalm 103:17

Eternal

Your kingdom is an everlasting kingdom, and your dominion endures through all generations. The LORD is faithful to all his promises and loving toward all he has made.

Psalm 145:13

Do you not know? Have you not heard? The LORD is the everlasting God, the Creator of the ends of the earth. He will not grow tired or weary, and his understanding no one can fathom.

Isaiah 40:28

> Once a man is united to God, how could he not live forever?
>
> C. S. Lewis

GOD IS COMPASSIONATE

Praise be to the God and Father
of our Lord Jesus Christ,
the Father of compassion
and the God of all comfort.

~ 2 Corinthians 1:3 ~

Compassionate

Our God is a God of infinite compassion and kindness. He understands all that we go through and sympathizes with our weakness and concerns. When we hurt, He is moved.

When we are troubled, He is sensitive to our predicament. He is not distant and far removed from our troubles. He came to live among us so that we could see how much He cares.

He comforts us when we need to be comforted. He understands us and sympathizes with us in our pain and hurt. We can take all our troubles to Him today and let the gentleness of His presence bring us comfort and peace.

From His Word

And the LORD said, "I will cause all my goodness to pass in front of you, and I will proclaim my name, the LORD, in your presence. I will have mercy on whom I will have mercy, and I will have compassion on whom I will have compassion."

Exodus 33:19

Have mercy on me, O God, according to your unfailing love; according to your great compassion blot out my transgressions.

Psalm 51:1

As a father has compassion on his children, so the LORD has compassion on those who fear him.

Psalm 103:13

I will tell of the kindnesses of the LORD, the deeds for which he is to be praised, according to all the LORD has done for us – yes, the many good things he has done for the house of Israel, according to his compassion and many kindnesses.

Isaiah 63:7

Compassionate

"Though the mountains be shaken and the hills be removed, yet my unfailing love for you will not be shaken nor my covenant of peace be removed," says the LORD, who has compassion on you.

Isaiah 54:10

Because of the LORD's great love we are not consumed, for his compassions never fail.

Lamentations 3:22

To the hurting, He is the Great Physician.

To the confused, He is the Light.

To the lost, He is the Way.

To the hungry, He is the Bread of Life.

To the thirsty, He is the Water of Life.

To the broken, He is the Balm of Gilead.

Calvin Miller

GOD IS OUR DEFENDER

Their Defender is strong;
he will take up
their case against you.
~ Proverbs 23:11 ~

Defender

In God we find shelter and a safe haven against the onslaughts of life. He has promised to protect us and be our shield and defender always. He is our refuge and source of security.

When the going gets tough you can flee to the safety of His protection. He will take up your cause and defend your position. That is why you need never fear. He is on your side and will never let you down.

He is stronger than anything or anyone. He champions those who are at the mercy of the oppressor of the righteous. Our God cares for us and defends us against all harm.

From His Word

For the LORD your God is God of gods and Lord of lords, the great God, mighty and awesome, who shows no partiality and accepts no bribes. He defends the cause of the fatherless and the widow, and loves the alien, giving him food and clothing.

Deuteronomy 10:17-18

You hear, O LORD, the desire of the afflicted; you encourage them, and you listen to their cry, defending the fatherless and the oppressed, in order that man, who is of the earth, may terrify no more.

Psalm 10:17-18

A father to the fatherless, a defender of widows, is God in his holy dwelling.

Psalm 68:5

Defend my cause and redeem me; preserve my life according to your promise.

Psalm 119:154

Defender

Yet their Redeemer is strong; the LORD Almighty is his name. He will vigorously defend their cause so that he may bring rest to their land, but unrest to those who live in Babylon.

Jeremiah 50:34

"He defended the cause of the poor and needy, and so all went well. Is that not what it means to know me?" declares the LORD.

Jeremiah 22:16

Do not look forward to the changes and chances of this life in fear; rather look to them with full hope that, as they arise, God, whose you are, will deliver you out of them. He is your keeper.

Francis de Sales

GOD IS FAITHFUL

Your love, O LORD,
reaches to the heavens,
your faithfulness to the skies.

~ Psalm 36:5 ~

Faithful

No matter what happens in the world around us, we can walk through life with confidence because our God is faithful.

When He speaks, we can know that what He says is the truth. He never breaks a promise and He never changes His mind.

He is trustworthy when all around us fails. He is dependable when all around us changes. He is faithful when all around us is like shifting sand.

He is not a man that He should lie. Not only does He speak the truth always, but He is absolute and eternal Truth. We can trust Him today, tomorrow and every day.

From His Word

Know therefore that the LORD your God is God; he is the faithful God, keeping his covenant of love to a thousand generations of those who love him and keep his commands.

Deuteronomy 7:9

Because of the LORD'S great love we are not consumed, for his compassions never fail. They are new every morning; great is your faithfulness.

Lamentations 3:22-23

God, who has called you into fellowship with his Son Jesus Christ our Lord, is faithful.

1 Corinthians 1:9

You know with all your heart and soul that not one of all the good promises the LORD your God gave you has failed. Every promise has been fulfilled; not one has failed.

Joshua 23:14

Faithful

Let us hold unswervingly to the hope we profess, for he who promised is faithful.

Hebrews 10:23

It is good to praise the LORD and make music to your name, O Most High, to proclaim your love in the morning and your faithfulness at night.

Psalm 92:1-2

Not to us, O LORD, not to us but to your name be the glory, because of your love and faithfulness.

Psalm 115:1

There is a living God; He has spoken in the Bible. He means what He says and will do all He has promised.

Hudson Taylor

GOD IS LIFE

The LORD God formed the man
from the dust of the ground
and breathed into his nostrils
the breath of life, and
the man became a living being.

~ Genesis 2:7 ~

Life

God is life. God is the source of all life – of all vitality, energy and strength. He truly pulsates life. It is only because of Him that everything else has life. We are alive because He is alive. The world exists only because He sustains it through His life.

The Bible teaches us that it is only as we come into a living relationship with God through Jesus Christ that we will begin to experience the fullness of life. It is only when we are rightly related to the source of life that we will truly live.

From His Word

Through him all things were made; without him nothing was made that has been made. In him was life, and that life was the light of men.

John 1:3-4

The Spirit of God has made me; the breath of the Almighty gives me life.

Job 33:4

"For God so loved the world that he gave his one and only Son, that whoever believes in him shall not perish but have eternal life."

John 3:16

God did this so that men would seek him and perhaps reach out for him and find him, though he is not far from each one of us. "For in him we live and move and have our being."

Acts 17:27-28

Life

With long life will I satisfy him and show him my salvation.

Psalm 91:16

When Christ, who is your life, appears, then you also will appear with him in glory.

Colossians 3:4

The LORD is the true God; he is the living God, the eternal King.

Jeremiah 10:10

> Time is short. Eternity is long. It is only reasonable that this short life be lived in the light of eternity.
>
> C. H. Spurgeon

God is Light

This is the message
we have heard from him
and declare to you:
God is light; in him
there is no darkness at all.

~ 1 John 1:5 ~

Light

The world is lost in the darkness of sin. We all want to find our way home, but in the darkness we stumble and fall. It is only when the Light of the world shines on the darkness in our lives that we are able to see our way clearly.

God shines the light of His glory all around us. It enables us to see morally, emotionally and spiritually.

Then we can find our way safely home through this dark world of sin.

Then we can appreciate the glory and beauty of all that God has done for us.

Let His light shine in your heart today and the darkness will flee before you.

From His Word

Every good and perfect gift is from above, coming down from the Father of the heavenly lights, who does not change like shifting shadows.

James 1:17

"I have come into the world as a light, so that no one who believes in me should stay in darkness."

John 12:46

God, the blessed and only Ruler, the King of kings and Lord of lords, who alone is immortal and who lives in unapproachable light, whom no one has seen or can see. To him be honor and might forever. Amen.

1 Timothy 6:15-16

The LORD is my light and my salvation – whom shall I fear? The LORD is the stronghold of my life – of whom shall I be afraid?

Psalm 27:1

Light

The city does not need the sun or the moon to shine on it, for the glory of God gives it light, and the Lamb is its lamp.

Revelation 21:23

For with you is the fountain of life; in your light we see light.

Psalm 36:9

A glimpse of the glory of God in the face of Jesus Christ causes in the heart a supreme, genuine love for God. This is because the divine light shows the excellent loveliness of God's nature.

Jonathan Edwards

GOD IS OUR FATHER

"Our Father in heaven,
hallowed be your name."
~ Matthew 6:9 ~

Father

Jesus revealed the Father-heart of God when He came to earth. No longer was God seen as remote and distant, but He became our Abba – our loving Father. He adopts us into His family and nurtures and cares for us as a father cares for his children.

No longer do we feel alone and abandoned in this world. We belong to His eternal family.

He created us, He loves us, and He provides for our every need.

He comforts us, and draws us into the intimacy of His warm embrace. He is all we could ever need in a Father.

From His Word

Because you are sons, God sent the Spirit of his Son into our hearts, the Spirit who calls out, "Abba, Father."

Galatians 4:6

"I will be a Father to you, and you will be my sons and daughters," says the Lord Almighty.

2 Corinthians 6:18

As a father has compassion on his children, so the LORD has compassion on those who fear him.

Psalm 103:13

Yet to all who received him, to those who believed in his name, he gave the right to become children of God – children born not of natural descent, nor of human decision or a husband's will, but born of God.

John 1:12-13

Father

How great is the love the Father has lavished on us, that we should be called children of God! And that is what we are!

1 John 3:1

Jesus replied, "If anyone loves me, he will obey my teaching. My Father will love him, and we will come to him and make our home with him."

John 14:23

> The God of the Christians is a God of love and consolation, a God who fills the souls and hearts of His own.
>
> Blaise Pascal

GOD IS GLORIOUS AND MAJESTIC

God, the blessed and only Ruler,
the King of kings and Lord of lords.

~ 1 Timothy 6:15 ~

Glorious and Majestic

God is king over the whole earth. The radiance of His glory shines forth in awesome splendor. He is the supreme ruler over all the earth. His reign will never cease and His kingdom will have no end.

Think of the most glorious kings and queens who have ever lived and their splendor fades into insignificance in the light of His glory.

He is awesome in majesty, breathtaking in loveliness, magnificent in beauty. Let us bow down before Him and give Him the glory due to His name.

From His Word

Lift up your heads, O you gates; lift them up, you ancient doors, that the King of glory may come in. Who is he, this King of glory? The LORD Almighty – he is the King of glory.

Psalm 24:9-10

Then I praised the Most High; I honored and glorified him who lives forever. His dominion is an eternal dominion; his kingdom endures from generation to generation.

Daniel 4:34

For God is the King of all the earth; sing to him a psalm of praise.

Psalm 47:7

Yours, O LORD, is the greatness and the power and the glory and the majesty and the splendor, for everything in heaven and earth is yours. Yours, O LORD, is the kingdom; you are exalted as head over all.

1 Chronicles 29:11

Glorious and Majestic

The LORD reigns, he is robed in majesty; the LORD is robed in majesty and is armed with strength.

Psalm 93:1

"Great and marvelous are your deeds, Lord God Almighty. Just and true are your ways, King of the ages."

Revelation 15:3

To the only God our Savior be glory, majesty, power and authority, through Jesus Christ our Lord, before all ages, now and forevermore! Amen.

Jude 25

There can be no kingdom of God in the world without the kingdom of God in our hearts.

Albert Schweitzer

GOD IS GOOD

And the LORD said, "I will cause all
my goodness to pass in front of you,
and I will proclaim my name,
the LORD, in your presence. I will have
mercy on whom I will have mercy,
and I will have compassion on
whom I will have compassion."

~ Exodus 33:19 ~

Good

God is good. Everything He does is a reflection of His moral excellence. But His goodness is not simply an abstract attribute. It refers to His attitude toward us – His kindness, goodwill and generosity that express His benevolence, love and mercy.

Because God is good, all the gifts He gives us are also good. Everything that is good comes from Him. He gives us good gifts to bless us.

All around us we see evidence of the goodness of God.

From His Word

His divine power has given us everything we need for life and godliness through our knowledge of him who called us by his own glory and goodness.

2 Peter 1:3

How great is your goodness, which you have stored up for those who fear you, which you bestow in the sight of men on those who take refuge in you.

Psalm 31:19

For the LORD God is a sun and shield; the LORD bestows favor and honor; no good thing does he withhold from those whose walk is blameless.

Psalm 84:11

We constantly pray for you, that our God may count you worthy of his calling, and that by his power he may fulfill every good purpose of yours and every act prompted by your faith.

2 Thessalonians 1:11

Good

Taste and see that the LORD is good; blessed is the man who takes refuge in him.

Psalm 34:8

For the LORD is good and his love endures forever; his faithfulness continues through all generations.

Psalm 100:5

Good and upright is the LORD; therefore he instructs sinners in his ways.

Psalm 25:8

All that is good, all that is true, all that is beautiful, all that is beneficent, be it great or small, be it perfect or fragmentary, natural as well as supernatural, moral as well as material, comes from God.

John Henry Newman

GOD IS TRANSCENDENT

The LORD has established
his throne in heaven,
and his kingdom rules over all.

~ Psalm 103:19 ~

Transcendent

Before there was anything, there was God. He created all that exists and He is above and beyond His creation.

No person on earth, no matter how important or significant he is, can measure up to God's greatness and magnificence. We bow before Him in adoration and wonder.

His wisdom and power are all-encompassing and go beyond any force in the universe. He rules the heavens and has everything under control.

He displays His glory through His creation and in the lives of those who worship Him.

From His Word

"For my thoughts are not your thoughts, neither are your ways my ways," declares the LORD. "As the heavens are higher than the earth, so are my ways higher than your ways and my thoughts than your thoughts."

Isaiah 55:8-9

Who is like the LORD our God, the One who sits enthroned on high, who stoops down to look on the heavens and the earth?

Psalm 113:5-6

"Can you fathom the mysteries of God? Can you probe the limits of the Almighty? They are higher than the heavens – what can you do? They are deeper than the depths of the grave – what can you know? Their measure is longer than the earth and wider than the sea."

Job 11:7-9

Transcendent

Great is the LORD and most worthy of praise; his greatness no one can fathom.

Psalm 145:3

Oh, the depth of the riches of the wisdom and knowledge of God! How unsearchable his judgments, and his paths beyond tracing out! "Who has known the mind of the Lord? Or who has been his counselor?"

Romans 11:33-34

"Who among the gods is like you, O LORD? Who is like you – majestic in holiness, awesome in glory, working wonders?"

Exodus 15:11

Oh, the fullness, pleasure, sheer excitement of knowing God on earth!

Jim Elliot

GOD IS GRACIOUS AND MERCIFUL

And he passed in front of Moses,
proclaiming, "The LORD, the LORD,
the compassionate and gracious
God, slow to anger, abounding
in love and faithfulness."

~ Exodus 34:6 ~

Gracious and Merciful

The Bible makes it very clear that God is the righteous Judge who hates evil. But the golden thread that runs through the Bible is the cord of His mercy. He is the merciful one who reaches out to sinners and forgives all those who turn to Him.

In His mercy, He withholds from us the punishment we deserve. In His grace, He blesses us with righteousness and goodness that we don't deserve.

Everything that we have and enjoy in life is because of the grace of God. Through His grace we are loved, upheld and cared for. If it were not for His mercy and grace, we would not be here!

From His Word

But you, O Lord, are a compassionate and gracious God, slow to anger, abounding in love and faithfulness.

Psalm 86:15

Yet the LORD longs to be gracious to you; he rises to show you compassion. For the LORD is a God of justice. Blessed are all who wait for him!

Isaiah 30:18

But he said to me, "My grace is sufficient for you, for my power is made perfect in weakness." Therefore I will boast all the more gladly about my weaknesses, so that Christ's power may rest on me.

2 Corinthians 12:9

Let us then approach the throne of grace with confidence, so that we may receive mercy and find grace to help us in our time of need.

Hebrews 4:16

Gracious and Merciful

To the praise of his glorious grace, which he has freely given us in the One he loves. In him we have redemption through his blood, the forgiveness of sins, in accordance with the riches of God's grace.

Ephesians 1:6-7

May our Lord Jesus Christ himself and God our Father, who loved us and by his grace gave us eternal encouragement and good hope, encourage your hearts and strengthen you in every good deed and word.

2 Thessalonians 2:16-17

Grace is the free, undeserved goodness and favor of God to mankind.

Matthew Henry

GOD EMANATES JOY

The joy of the LORD
is your strength.

~ Nehemiah 8:10 ~

Joy

God is not only an awesome ruler, He is also a God of joy who delights in His children and in giving them gifts.

When we dwell in His presence our lives will be characterized by joy because He is the fountain of all true joy.

As we grow closer to Him, our capacity for joy is increased and we share in His delight for all the good things He has made.

God finds great pleasure and enjoyment in those who love Him and turn to Him and walk in His ways. The Bible tells us that He rejoices over us. And we in turn can rejoice in Him.

From His Word

The LORD made the heavens. Splendor and majesty are before him; strength and joy in his dwelling place.

1 Chronicles 16:26-27

You have made known to me the path of life; you will fill me with joy in your presence, with eternal pleasures at your right hand.

Psalm 16:11

The LORD your God is with you, he is mighty to save. He will take great delight in you, he will quiet you with his love, he will rejoice over you with singing.

Zephaniah 3:17

You have loved righteousness and hated wickedness; therefore God, your God, has set you above your companions by anointing you with the oil of joy.

Hebrews 1:9

Joy

They feast on the abundance of your house; you give them drink from your river of delights.

Psalm 36:8

For the LORD takes delight in his people; he crowns the humble with salvation.

Psalm 149:4

You have filled my heart with greater joy than when their grain and new wine abound.

Psalm 4:7

No matter what looms ahead, if you can eat today, enjoy the sunlight today, mix good cheer with friends today, enjoy it, and bless God for it.

Henry Ward Beecher

God is our Redeemer

I know that my Redeemer lives,
and that in the end
he will stand upon the earth.

~ Job 19:25 ~

Redeemer

Every person who has ever lived on earth has strayed from the paths of God and has been caught in the bondage of sin. We need someone to save us, to rescue us from this bondage. God could have sent angels to save us. He could have stayed in heaven and caused the earth to shake and so set us free.

But He chose to come down Himself and share in our sufferings. He opened the prison doors and led the way to freedom. Out of His great love He paid the price that was required to buy us back.

Our salvation depends entirely on Him. All we need to do is believe in Him and receive His gift of grace.

From His Word

Yet their Redeemer is strong; the LORD Almighty is his name. He will vigorously defend their cause so that he may bring rest to their land, but unrest to those who live in Babylon.

Jeremiah 50:34

And the ransomed of the LORD will return. They will enter Zion with singing; everlasting joy will crown their heads. Gladness and joy will overtake them, and sorrow and sighing will flee away.

Isaiah 35:10

But now, this is what the LORD says he who created you, O Jacob, he who formed you, O Israel: "Fear not, for I have redeemed you; I have summoned you by name; you are mine."

Isaiah 43:1

"For even the Son of Man did not come to be served, but to serve, and to give his life as a ransom for many."

Mark 10:45

Redeemer

In him we have redemption through his blood, the forgiveness of sins, in accordance with the riches of God's grace.

Ephesians 1:7

He did not enter by means of the blood of goats and calves; but he entered the Most Holy Place once for all by his own blood, having obtained eternal redemption.

Hebrews 9:12

Come and see the victories of the cross. Christ's wounds are thy healings, His agonies thy repose, His conflicts thy conquests, His groans thy songs, His pains thine ease, His shame thy glory, His death thy life, His sufferings, thy salvation.

Matthew Henry

GOD IS UNCHANGING

"I the LORD do not change.
So you, O descendants of Jacob,
are not destroyed."

~ Malachi 3:6 ~

Unchanging

God has no beginning and no end. He is in all ways and at all times absolutely perfect and does not need to change or grow or become more than He is. He alone fills eternity and is unchanging.

God is constant, dependable and steadfast. His love does not waver. His kindness does not falter. His goodness does not fluctuate. His compassion has no end and His supplies are limitless.

God loved you yesterday, He loves you today and He will love you tomorrow. On that you can depend.

From His Word

The grass withers and the flowers fall, but the word of our God stands forever.

Isaiah 40:8

God is not a man, that he should lie, nor a son of man, that he should change his mind. Does he speak and then not act? Does he promise and not fulfill? I have received a command to bless; he has blessed, and I cannot change it.

Numbers 23:19-20

But the plans of the LORD stand firm forever, the purposes of his heart through all generations.

Psalm 33:11

Remember the former things, those of long ago; I am God, and there is no other; I am God, and there is none like me. I make known the end from the beginning, from ancient times, what is still to come. I say: My purpose will stand, and I will do all that I please.

Isaiah 46:9-10

Unchanging

"This is what the LORD says – Israel's King and Redeemer, the LORD Almighty: I am the first and I am the last; apart from me there is no God."

Isaiah 44:6

He has delivered us from such a deadly peril, and he will deliver us. On him we have set our hope that he will continue to deliver us.

2 Corinthians 1:10

For he is the living God and he endures forever; his kingdom will not be destroyed, his dominion will never end.

Daniel 6:26

Trust the past to God's mercy, the present to God's love and the future to God's providence.

Augustine of Hippo

GOD IS JUST

He is the Rock,
his works are perfect,
and all his ways are just.
A faithful God who does no wrong,
upright and just is he.

~ Deuteronomy 32:4 ~

Just

A judge is appointed to evaluate a case impartially and with absolute fairness. But only God is able to fully understand every aspect of every situation in the world. He alone understands not only all the facts, but also the motivations of the heart. And so His judgment is impartial, fair and based on truth.

God will, on the final day of judgment, right all wrongs and judge each person according to His standards. He will ensure that justice prevails. Therefore we do not need to become enraged and bitter about the unfairness in the world.

We can leave the final judgment to God and do what we can in His name to ensure justice and righteousness are seen on the earth.

From His Word

Far be it from you to do such a thing – to kill the righteous with the wicked, treating the righteous and the wicked alike. Far be it from you! Will not the Judge of all the earth do right?

Genesis 18:25

Then I heard the angel in charge of the waters say: "You are just in these judgments, you who are and who were, the Holy One, because you have so judged."

Revelation 16:5

They will sing before the LORD, for he comes, he comes to judge the earth. He will judge the world in righteousness and the peoples in his truth.

Psalm 96:13

Your throne, O God, will last for ever and ever; a scepter of justice will be the scepter of your kingdom.

Psalm 45:6

Just

My shield is God Most High, who saves the upright in heart. God is a righteous judge.

Psalm 7:10-11

The LORD reigns forever; he has established his throne for judgment. He will judge the world in righteousness; he will govern the peoples with justice.

Psalm 9:7-8

> God examines both rich and poor, not according to their lands and houses, but according to the riches of their hearts.
>
> Augustine of Hippo

GOD IS LONG-SUFFERING

The LORD is compassionate
and gracious, slow to anger,
abounding in love.

~ Psalm 103:8 ~

Long-suffering

God is infinitely patient. He watches over us when we stumble and fall and He is always ready to help us up.

So often we try to do things our way. Stubbornly we dig in our heels and ignore God. But He waits for us, watching over us with tender care. His pattern with us has been His way with mankind since the beginning of time.

He waits patiently for people to turn to Him and experience His love and care. He woos us and lures us with His love and kindness and does not grow impatient with our shortcomings. He treats us with gentleness and compassion.

From His Word

The Lord is not slow in keeping his promise, as some understand slowness. He is patient with you, not wanting anyone to perish, but everyone to come to repentance.

2 Peter 3:9

May the God who gives endurance and encouragement give you a spirit of unity among yourselves as you follow Christ Jesus.

Romans 15:5

Love is patient, love is kind.

1 Corinthians 13:4

Or do you show contempt for the riches of his kindness, tolerance and patience, not realizing that God's kindness leads you toward repentance?

Romans 2:4

Long-suffering

God presented him as a sacrifice of atonement, through faith in his blood. He did this to demonstrate his justice, because in his forbearance he had left the sins committed beforehand unpunished.

Romans 3:25

But you, O Lord, are a compassionate and gracious God, slow to anger, abounding in love and faithfulness.

Psalm 86:15

> When God ripens apples, He isn't in a hurry and doesn't make a noise.
>
> D. Jackman

GOD IS OMNIPRESENT

This is what the LORD says:
"Heaven is my throne,
and the earth is my footstool.
Where is the house
you will build for me?
Where will my resting place be?"

~ Isaiah 66:1 ~

Omnipresent

God is not bound by the limits of space and time. He sees all things all the time all over the world. There is no place we can go where God is not present. He is always thinking about us.

Everything in the world is equally present to God and He is in control of everything at all times.

Knowing that He is always everywhere brings great comfort to our hearts because it assures us that His presence will not fail to protect, soothe, guard and guide us.

From His Word

"His eyes are on the ways of men; he sees their every step. There is no dark place, no deep shadow, where evildoers can hide."

Job 34:21-22

"But will God really dwell on earth? The heavens, even the highest heaven, cannot contain you. How much less this temple I have built!"

1 Kings 8:27

Where can I go from your Spirit? Where can I flee from your presence? If I go up to the heavens, you are there; if I make my bed in the depths, you are there. If I rise on the wings of the dawn, if I settle on the far side of the sea, even there your hand will guide me.

Psalm 139:7-10

For the eyes of the LORD range throughout the earth to strengthen those whose hearts are fully committed to him.

2 Chronicles 16:9

Omnipresent

The God who made the world and everything in it is the Lord of heaven and earth and does not live in temples built by hands. And he is not served by human hands, as if he needed anything, because he himself gives all men life and breath and everything else. From one man he made every nation of men, that they should inhabit the whole earth; and he determined the times set for them and the exact places where they should live. God did this so that men would seek him and perhaps reach out for him and find him, though he is not far from each one of us.

Acts 17:24-27

God is always near you and with you; leave Him not alone.

Brother Lawrence

GOD IS OMNISCIENT

Nothing in all creation
is hidden from God's sight.
Everything is uncovered
and laid bare
before the eyes of him
to whom we must give account.

~ Hebrews 4:13 ~

Omniscient

God knows all things. He knows everything that is both actual and possible. He knows the dramatic and world-changing things, as well as the minute details that seem so insignificant – like when a sparrow falls or the number of hairs you have on your head.

Not only does God know the things that happen, He also knows the thoughts and intents of the heart. Because He is beyond time, God knows all that has happened, is happening and will happen in the future.

God's knowledge is eternal and beyond our understanding. His thoughts are far above ours. We can trust Him to do the right thing always because He knows the end from the beginning.

From His Word

Hear from heaven, your dwelling place. Forgive and act; deal with each man according to all he does, since you know his heart (for you alone know the hearts of all men).

1 Kings 8:39

From heaven the LORD looks down and sees all mankind; from his dwelling place he watches all who live on earth – he who forms the hearts of all, who considers everything they do.

Psalm 33:13-15

Remember the former things, those of long ago; I am God, and there is no other; I am God, and there is none like me. I make known the end from the beginning, from ancient times, what is still to come. I say: My purpose will stand, and I will do all that I please. From the east I summon a bird of prey; from a far-off land, a man to fulfill my purpose. What I have said, that will I bring about; what I have planned, that will I do.

Isaiah 46:9-11

Omniscient

God understands the way to it and he alone knows where it dwells, for he views the ends of the earth and sees everything under the heavens.

Job 28:23-24

The eyes of the LORD are everywhere, keeping watch on the wicked and the good.

Proverbs 15:3

Oh, the depth of the riches of the wisdom and knowledge of God! How unsearchable his judgments, and his paths beyond tracing out!

Romans 11:33

There are three things that only God knows: the beginning of things, the cause of things and the end of things.

Welsh Proverb

GOD IS SOVEREIGN

Adonai

To him who loves us
and has freed us from our sins
by his blood, and has made us
to be a kingdom and priests
to serve his God and Father –
to him be glory and power
for ever and ever! Amen.

~ Revelation 1:5-6 ~

Sovereign

God created the world and all that is in it and He has sovereign control over it.

God has the supreme right to rule the universe because He is the true owner and master of it.

God has the authority to do what pleases Him. And because He is good, upright and just, what pleases Him is always right.

We need not fear because our lives and the destiny of the whole universe are in the hands of the sovereign and almighty Lord.

From His Word

And Hezekiah prayed to the LORD: "O LORD, God of Israel, enthroned between the cherubim, you alone are God over all the kingdoms of the earth. You have made heaven and earth."

2 Kings 19:15

Many are the plans in a man's heart, but it is the LORD's purpose that prevails.

Proverbs 19:21

And we know that in all things God works for the good of those who love him, who have been called according to his purpose.

Romans 8:28

The LORD does whatever pleases him, in the heavens and on the earth, in the seas and all their depths. He makes clouds rise from the ends of the earth; he sends lightning with the rain and brings out the wind from his storehouses.

Psalm 135:6-7

Sovereign

In him we were also chosen, having been pre-destined according to the plan of him who works out everything in conformity with the purpose of his will.

Ephesians 1:11

He is before all things, and in him all things hold together.

Colossians 1:17

The earth is the LORD's, and everything in it, the world, and all who live in it.

Psalm 24:1

To want all that God wants, always to want it, for all occasions and without reservations, this is the kingdom of God.

François Fénelon

GOD IS WISE

To the only wise God
be glory forever
through Jesus Christ! Amen.

~ Romans 16:27 ~

Wise

All knowledge and wisdom reside in God.

He understands the deep things of life – He knows how the world was created and He knows how you were formed in your mother's womb.

He has all the knowledge to sustain the universe and to direct and govern our lives. He has all insight, understanding and wisdom.

We should always trust Him to know what is best for us!

From His Word

It is because of him that you are in Christ Jesus, who has become for us wisdom from God – that is, our righteousness, holiness and redemption.

1 Corinthians 1:30

But the wisdom that comes from heaven is first of all pure; then peace-loving, considerate, submissive, full of mercy and good fruit, impartial and sincere. Peacemakers who sow in peace raise a harvest of righteousness.

James 3:17-18

By wisdom the LORD laid the earth's foundations, by understanding he set the heavens in place.

Proverbs 3:19

His intent was that now, through the church, the manifold wisdom of God should be made known to the rulers and authorities in the heavenly realms.

Ephesians 3:10

Wise

He has filled him with the Spirit of God, with skill, ability and knowledge in all kinds of craft.

Exodus 35:31

My purpose is that they may be encouraged in heart and united in love, so that they may have the full riches of complete understanding, in order that they may know the mystery of God, namely, Christ, in whom are hidden all the treasures of wisdom and knowledge.

Colossians 2:2-3

> The truly wise are those whose souls are in Christ.
>
> St. Ambrose

OTHER BOOKS
IN THIS RANGE

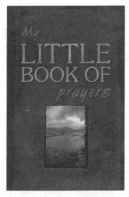

1-86920-061-6   1-86920-062-4

1-86920-064-0

1-86920-063-2

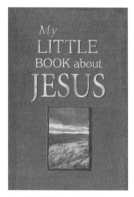

1-86920-541-3